WHIMSIES & WONDERS

Finding Joy Within the Chaos

MARCIE SWIFT

INTRODUCTION

Years ago, in my 30s, I purchased a thick, small book filled with quotes and images of beauty from wisdom teachers around the world and throughout time. Once a day, I would turn a page, read something new, rest in the image and open my heart to inspiration. That book has long since found its way to other homes, other hearts, but this morning, absorbing the wonder and insight of *Whimsies & Wonders*, I found myself resting in the same way I rested so long ago—into a moment out of time, where possibilities swirled around me. The world felt larger and welcoming, and my own body calmed and was healed.

Marcie Swift's work is an offering of the highest kind, one born out of the lived knowledge that emerges from a broken moment faced with courage, an offering of generosity, spirit and imagination. There is beauty here, and innocence, an invitation to both rest and rejoice, and a surprising calmness in the face of illness. I found myself uplifted by its color and delightful swirls—wishing I could be that person held by so much iridescence—and yet grounded in the simple guidance she has culled from facing cancer and the fragility of life. Any one page offers so much, and upon finishing, I choose to start again, this time with a warm, full mug and a spot in the sun, eager to see which teaching feels the most resonant for the day. With this book in hand, you will want to do the same.

Susan Sontag, during her experience of breast cancer treatment, reminded us that we are always navigating the kingdom of the ill and the kingdom of the well at the same time. That, even in moments of seeming health, our bodies are aging, shifting and addressing potential illness in hidden and not-so-hidden ways. As such, we are invited, sometimes forced, to consider how we might navigate the two kingdoms. Marcie Swift has given us a remarkable choice here— leading us to consider that we might just make our way through by allowing all parts of ourselves to remember their vital life force: our bodies for certain, our hearts and minds, our imaginings, and our spirits open to mystery and synchronicity and unexpected grace.

That we might find joy along the journey of illness is a potent consideration.

That illness may not be the whole of us at any one time and that our life force is always present, even with multiple cancers, is a beam of hope.

That we might share that joy, without reservation, through color and play and language that is of itself life-giving, is a goodness, a beneficence of great value.

My day is better having read this work . . . yours will be, too.

And if we follow her guidance and attend to the heart of this work—its gladness and uplift and care—with an open mind, we will experience respite and reinvigoration and a kind of quiet rejoicing. And isn't that exactly what we are all longing for in the face of all we are asked to carry?

Maria Sirois, Psy.D., is the author of *The Generous Exchange: How Attention to Beauty, Goodness and Excellence Restores Us and Our World*; *A Short Course in Happiness After Loss*; and *Every Day Counts.*

FOREWORD

This book arrives at a particularly opportune time. So many changes are occurring throughout our society, and they are having a profound impact on how we think, feel and live our lives. As much as ever before, we need an abiding sense of hopefulness and a deeper connection with ourselves and others. We also need to smile and laugh and open our hearts, with grace, to the abundant wonders around us. Marcie's beautiful book enables us to accomplish all these things, and many more.

I have known Marcie for nearly 50 years, and this book represents so many aspects of her life. She is a dedicated athlete who swims and kayaks, a musician who weaves exquisite melodies on her harp, a therapist who has listened to and offered sage advice to her many patients, and a lover of people, places and dogs. She is also a cancer survivor who acknowledges her "harrowing journey" of treatments, which she used to become clearer and stronger and "create pathways to joy and serenity." In so many ways, Marcie is an inspiration for hopefulness and courage to everyone who knows her and embraces her book. And her inspiration is presented on every page.

The paintings represent Marcie's interpretations of people and places, so often depicted with vibrant colors and dreamlike designs. Some of her paintings tell seemingly explicit stories, such as of two people with a large heart between them, or riding on an elephant, or tenderly holding each other. Other paintings depict Marcie embracing life—which can represent our lives—as she lies in a kayak, with dragonflies sharing their energy with her, or as she reaches, arms spread, to greet a large bird or the sun or autumn's multicolored leaves. Still other paintings portray Marcie's positive spirit and enthusiasm, such as the ones about an inner child or a woman in a bathing suit diving into the blue-gray water.

What makes Marcie's book even more powerful and helpful are the words of wisdom and guidance that accompany each painting. We can react to each painting, with joy or curiosity or awe, and then be prompted and nurtured by her simple insights that acknowledge our humanness and what we really need. As Marcie so wisely observes, "by imagining the unimaginable we create miracles of joy." Further, as "we find ourselves living through increasingly disorienting and chaotic times," what she gives us, with so much love and generosity of spirit, is a wise partner on our journey. I read Marcie's book and reflected on my life, and I knew she was with me every step of the way.

Rick Gregg has been a healthcare management consultant, director and CEO of Kripalu Center for Yoga & Health, and interim CEO of Community Health Programs/CHP Berkshires in Massachusetts. Currently he is a distinguished instructor of healthcare administration at Suffolk University in Boston.

PREFACE

May this small book lift your spirits and remind you of the preciousness of your existence. In the bleakest times, may you be wrapped in a cocoon of hopefulness, fortitude and wisdom.

In 2001, I was diagnosed with the first of four cancers caused by a genetic mutation in my BRCA1 gene. This began a harrowing journey of many surgeries and long rounds of potent chemotherapy.

On each day of chemo, I rose to play my Celtic harp, kept at the foot of my bed, and I forced myself to use our treadmill, which I hoped would keep me strong.

I learned that devastating news can also create pathways to joy and serenity. It was not always easy, but somehow possible.

In the year 2020, at the beginning of the COVID pandemic, I began a spiritually enriching painting journey with artist Elisabeth Moss, who led a weekly art sangha. Each Monday, our small group met online to meditate and paint. It was Elisabeth's steadfast inspiration and nurturing of my creative endeavors that led to each of the paintings in this book.

As I write, we find ourselves living through increasingly disorienting and chaotic times. My hope is that you will find comfort and delight in these pages. May your days be fortified by beauty, love and joy.

My deepest gratitude is for my loving and wise husband, Gordon, and the many friends who accompanied us on the long path to well-being. Heartfelt thanks to beloved friend Theresa Sundt, artist and color therapist, who struck the spark within me to create this book.

Marcie Swift

We were brought here to live
with wonder and awe—
to fan the flames of love
for all living creatures.

Immerse yourself each day
in nature's bounties.

When we open each of our senses,
we let go of fear
and embrace our whole selves.

There is so much emphasis
on being present and in the moment.

However,
sometimes, allowing ourselves
to drift into the past and future
in a dreamy way
can unlock the deepest secrets
and wishes in our hearts.

Nurturing your body and mind
as though you are
your own young child
can fortify you
during times of deep discomfort
and distress.

Love someone.

Maybe this is why
we were given life.

Our journey in this Great Mystery
is eased when shared
with a loving companion
who supports us with comfort
and wisdom.

With so much unknown
in our days ahead,
the presence and constancy of love
builds our resilience
and embraces us with hope.

This is a true story:

One day, in the aftermath of ending a very difficult relationship, I sat at my kitchen table, dreaming of what a future relationship might look like. I imagined my dad's loving kindness and compassion, his wholehearted belief in and support of me, and his sensitivity and keen intellect. I let this image sink deep into my heart. One month later, I met the man who possessed all of these fine qualities. He continues, after 33 years, to be my soul mate.

Solitude can be a balm
to our souls
and a healing prayer.
Rest and listen
to the wisdom of the inner voice
before venturing forth.

Believe in the power
of fantasy and awe.

A daily dose
can quell anxiety
and depression.

Sometimes, we forget to slow down and drift into union with the Great Mystery.

This is my true story: A decade ago, I was in treatment for cancer when I learned that new test results showed signs of another cancer. Fearful, I paddled out onto our lake in my orange kayak and pulled into a quiet cove. I leaned back and let go of my paddles, crying out, "Oh God, what will become of me?"

At that very moment, more than 30 dragonflies and damselflies covered me from my neck to my toes with protective energy. I felt their immediate reassurance that all would be well.

Sometimes a brief fling
into delicious fantasy and daydreaming
can reveal creative solutions
to our deepest conflicts.

With a resting mind,
the floodgates open
with grace and promise.

We untangle the knots of worry
and open to possibilities.

Simply slowing down
and leaving our home
to touch, see and smell
the wonders of nature
can lead to immediate awe
and a completely unique perspective.

It is easy to trap ourselves
in repetitive and self-defeating thoughts.

In a matter of moments,
we can walk away
into a different reality
and let nature begin her healing.

When we pause
and savor
and let go of our obsessive strivings,
we can touch the Divine Mystery
that is always simmering
beneath the surface.

At these moments,
we see reflections
of our truest nature.

In the stillness
of the darkest nights
I perceive the gentlest stirrings
of a new life.

I have no choice
but to surrender.

I only asked for wonder
and God gave it to me.

M Swift

Deep inside your soul
lies an inner child
crying for your attention.

Run to her!

Each day I am reminded
of the abundant and delicious power
of my labradoodle's adoration
and affection.

So often, his endless energy, antics
and attention
cheer and heal me.

Move your body
with joy and grace,
and dance yourself
into a delicious swoon
of happiness.

What helps to make us grow
and dampens the voice of self-criticism?

Flowing inside sacred spaces
in the present moment
heals our hearts
and nurtures our journey.

Sometimes we need to do
absolutely nothing
in order to begin to do
anything.

Our bonds with others
create threads of support
that insulate us
from loneliness and despair.

Without them,
we may perish.

While the world may swirl
and twist all about us,
there is a deep center of grounding
that throbs within our hearts.

We can listen to its beat
and breathe.

Build your home
on the foundations
of loving kindness
and devotion.
These are our sacred sanctuaries.

As much in awe as I,
this tiny being
greeted me in my garden
one summer day.

He glowed with curiosity and intelligence,
examining me
as carefully as I did him.

I imagined him
flying back to his nest later
to look me up in his Human Species book
for quick identification!

There is magic
in the woods
if only we would stop
to look and listen.

What miracles await
those who seek them!

Far from the coast,
I can see things
clearly.

Opening wide
to the creations
of the universe,
I am grounded
in Deep Union.

Rejoice
in every breath
and in the miracle
of your creation.

Sometimes
we just need
to dive in!

Dampening the voice
of self-doubt and worry
can free us to become
our Whole Selves.

By imagining
the unimaginable,
we create miracles
of joy!

We are one—
any estrangement
from this awareness
brings a withering of the soul.

Our planet is so rich
in its diversity.

Our ability to respect
all forms of life
will shape our destiny.

Who can stand
before the enormity
of our universe
and not be humbled?

We can always walk
toward new horizons
and immerse our spirits
in wonder, novelty
and surprise.

What a miracle
to find ourselves alive
each new day,
waiting to discover
mysteries and treasures.

How we resist turbulence
and change in our daily lives!

Yet by surrendering,
we face the opportunity
to become our most authentic
and self-actualized
selves.

How quickly
we forget
that we are children
of the earth,
born to surrender
to love and beauty.

Even from the depths
of despair,
we can rise above
and gather
stardust.

Soul mates are rare
and difficult to find.
If discovered,
never
ever
let them go.

The more this world spins,
the more I long for stillness.

It awaits me
with open arms.

Only in our longing
and wounded vulnerability
may we find our way
home.

There is magic
above and below the sea
that waits
for open eyes
and hearts.

Myriads of journeys
rely upon the uplifting
and inspiration of others.

In flight, the wisdom of others
can guide us to our North Star.

The launch and the landing
are equally graced
by thoughtful selection of mentors
in all aspects of our life.

Choosing role models carefully
illuminates our path.

This crazy mixed-up world
behooves us to escape
into fantasy and delight.

How else can we rise
to meet each day?

In tumultuous and chaotic times,
it is easy to lose your vision
and balance.

Find safe and stable sanctuaries
and practices
to build resilience
in mind, body and spirit.

Spend far more time in these practices
than in the chaos.

Maintain your boundaries!

Welcome the wonder
of this day
into your heart.

May beauty and peace
wrap you
in hope and gratitude.

Marcie Swift's paintings are available for purchase; contact her at marcieswift@msn.com.